DAMEON GIBBS

Him, Her & God

GIBBS PUBLISHING

GPC

CONGLOMERATE

First published by Gibbs Publishing Conglomerate 2025

Second edition

ISBN: 978-1-966856-05-4

Advisor: Tiffany Gibbs

This book was professionally typeset on Reedsy.
Find out more at reedsy.com

We dedicate this book to all the individuals fighting for their marriages and relationships. May the Lord give you the strength to continue in His ways.

Marriage is honorable in all, and the bed undefiled.

HEBREWS 13:4

Contents

Foreword

This idea of Him, Her, and God came to me in a dream one night. In this dream, there was a woman having marriage issues, and she asked for my counsel on a particular matter of what she should do. I do not remember the exact details of what I said to her, but I do remember encouraging her to do her best to maintain their marriage. The advice seemed to have calmed her down. She asked for my name, number, and if I could continue to counsel her one-on-one.

Let me clarify that this particular lady was wearing a deep red dress and was very attractive, even in the dream, I could feel a side of me wanting to say, "Sure." However, my spirit promptly answered, *No.* After giving my clear response, I continued explaining to her that I was a married man and how this would not be the proper thing for a married man to do.

Now, the next thing that happened was amazing. I came out of the dream, and at this time it was 4:00 am. I looked over at my wife, as I was eager to tell her about the dream. I felt great, joyful, and encouraged by what I witnessed in the dream. However, being that she was deep asleep, I reached over, grabbed the notepad I kept by my bedside, and filled an entire page with my experience, so as not to forget.

It felt like I had passed a test. The amazing thing about all of this was that, after waking up, God then gave me the revelation concerning Man, Woman, and Himself. Before this dream, I had never studied this aspect of God's word on marriage. And as I was writing my notes that night, I began to understand how Bible-based relationships and marriage should function versus what the world says they should be.

I believe the teachings contained in this book are simple, yet revealing enough to open the eyes and hearts of those who desire to improve their relationship with their spouse and, more importantly, with God the Father. The idea is that both man and woman have standards that they must abide by within their godly relationship. These standards were established for the husband and wife by our Lord at the beginning of time. Therefore, I believe as long as marriages abide by these standards, our relationship with both our spouse and God will be in harmony. I am not saying troubles will not arise, but by understanding our place within the marriage, we will recognize issues and act accordingly. Why? Because we understand the standards He has given us.

In this book, I will be providing a husband's perspective of marriage according to the scriptures, while my beloved wife will provide a woman's perspective of a biblical marriage. May the words contained in this book bless, encourage, and help to strengthen your holy union.

Dameon Gibbs

Preface

There have been many books discussing marriage, along with works that explain the thoughts of both men and women. Yet there will always be one book that outranks them all, including the one in which you are reading now. If you really desire to understand marriage and to understand how the opposite sex is meant to live, then I encourage you to dive into the Holy scriptures, which are written by He who knows all things.

It is written in **John 2:24**, "But Jesus did not commit himself unto them because he knew all *men*." The word "*men*" written at the end of John 2:24 is written in italics, thus it was inserted into the scriptures by the translator in hopes of providing more clarification for readers. Jesus knew all, He knows all. He knows the heart of all. Know, or its equivalent word, knowledge, is defined as the ability to perceive all, any, every, and the whole.[1]

Being that He knows all about all, whether man or woman, it is best we totally rely upon Him for the source of this knowledge. This does not mean we should not read additional material on the subject. I am simply stating that we should not neglect the

---

[1] see Strgs#1097 & 3956

one who truly knows the purpose of marriage because He was the one who created and initiated it.

The Bible is the only work on earth that can explain every thought and intention of both man and woman. And by having an understanding of both sexes, the Bible can teach us how the two were meant to coexist as one being upon their unification through marriage.

Acknowledgments

In every case, we first give thanks to our Lord and Savior Jesus the Christ. Without Him, none of this would be possible. Jesus' Blood, Spirit, and Word have forever changed us, granting us a life that we never thought possible.

We give special thanks to our Pastors, Donald and Judith Peart, for being our spiritual parents. May God continue to bless you with all spiritual blessings.

And last but not least, we would like to thank all our friends and family who have supported us through this process. God bless you all.

HIM

Giving Up Distractions

Genesis 2:18-25 KJV:

18. And the Lord God said, It is not good that the man should be alone; I will make him an help meet for him. **19**. And out of the ground the Lord God formed every beast of the field and every fowl of the air; and brought them unto Adam to see what he would call them: and every living creature, that was the name thereof. **20**. And Adam gave names to all cattle, and to the fowl of the air, and to every beast of the field; but for Adam there was not found an help meet for him. **21**. And the Lord God caused a deep sleep to fall upon Adam, and he slept: and he took one of his ribs, and closed up the flesh instead thereof; **22**. And the rib, which the Lord God had taken from man, made he a woman, and brought her unto the man. **23**. And Adam Said, This is now bone of my bones, and flesh of my flesh: she shall be called Woman, because she was taken out of Man. 24. Therefore shall a man leave his father and his mother, and shall cleave unto his wife: and they shall be one flesh. **25**. And they were both naked, the man and his wife, and were not ashamed.

For a man to realize and tap into the potential that lies within his help meet, he must first do one of the hardest things a man can do within a relationship. This thing that a man must turn away from is distractions, not some, but all distractions that are before him. This is the first principle the Lord shared with me: the necessity for man to give up distractions.

The scripture states that after God created man, He then put man in a position to work.[2] However, God determined it was not good for man to work alone; thus, He made beasts of the field and fowl of the air to be a help meet for Adam.[3] Within that batch of creation, Adam did not identify with any of the creatures as being his suitable help meet. As the scripture reads, *"But for Adam there was not found* [lit. one to take hold of, to exist][4] *an help meet for him."*

Since Adam did not see a help meet that he wanted to take hold of or wanted to exist with, God caused a deep sleep to fall upon him. God removed one of his ribs. This rib was then used to create Adam's true and only help meet.

The word "sleep" in **Genesis 2:21** is an interesting word. It does mean a deep sleep, lethargy, and trance, but it comes from a root word meaning to stun and death.[5] In other words, Adam had to first die to himself in order to see the one who was

---

[2] see **Genesis 2:6-15**

[3] Make in **Genesis 2:18** is the Hebrew word *âśâh* (aw-saw), meaning to do, accomplish, advance, appoint, fashion, fulfill, prepare and maintain, see Strgs#6213

[4] see Strgs#4672

[5] see Strgs#8639 & 7290

3

created for him and have her come into being. What does dying mean, or what does it look like? Man dying means to die to self ambitions for the sake of working in the Lord's garden. Stated differently, dying is working in the ministry of building His kingdom. It would be giving up that which would please oneself, in order to perform the necessary tasks to establish the Lord's kingdom.

However, although man can name things and work the fields, he will never be able to do it himself. Thus, he will never get to see his help meet until he dies to self, allowing God to remove the bone and purify him.[6]

With man's rib in hand, the Lord built[7] the woman and brought her to the man. Ribs in **Genesis 2:21** are defined as a door or a timber.[8] Even in this interaction of God's holy plan for the relationship, you can see the importance of balance. Yes, man was first, and man may be the head of the house, yet man must know how to treat women, the same as he is treated by his head.[9] But man cannot work alone; however, man can find strength in the very thing taken out of him. He can find entrances into other aspects of life if he is able to locate and obtain a help meet.

Eve was created from bone, which is the strongest and hardest substance in the human body. Without it, the body would be immobile and weak. How ironic it is that the Lord chose to build the woman out of that which supports the man internally. Do you see and understand the implication of women being

---

[6] see closed up - to shut up, surrender, repair, pure, deliver see Strgs#5462

[7] made in **Genesis 2:22** translate as built, see Strgs#1129

[8] see Strgs#6763

[9] compare **1 Cor. 11:3**

made of bone?

The ribs protect and hold together (support) all man's vital organs; this is the very definition of help meet, which is to aid, surround, and protect.[10] Along with women being a help meet by being able to aid, surround, and protect mankind. We will also come to understand in later chapters that women are also the support that binds and keeps the household together.

By allowing the woman to be his support, a man comes to have a help meet who could support him not only internally (spiritually) but externally (physically) as well. The woman is a part of a man's strength in the relationship, and without her, he would be significantly less mobile and weaker. Just as the human body would lack both strength and mobility without having the strength of the skeletal system. The skeletal system brings structure and strength to the body, so likewise, women bring into the relationship with man.

Although the Lord had given man the earth and beasts to dominate, man had to recognize he needed help. It is very much true that men like to tackle things and situations alone, and I am personally guilty of this. Yet like myself, I had to learn to depend on my help meet to aid me in life. To meditate on this situation of needing help, God determined to provide this help in the form of women. So marriage and relationship are not based on how man perceives or envisions it, no, it's God's perception of marriage.

Eve was created and placed there in the garden to help strengthen Adam (Eve was created from his bone after all), which would enable him to accomplish the work of dominating the earth. Husbands cannot do the work of the garden alone;

---

[10] see Strgs#5828 and 5826

husbands must recognize and acknowledge the ability lying inside their wife, to assist them. It was never the Lord's intention for man or woman to work alone doing the ministry, or to raise a household.

With this, I would like to mention that not every man or woman will choose or become married, nothing wrong or unrighteousness about this. For Jesus was not physically married, but was spiritually married to the church. So likewise, many may not be or become physically married but are spiritually married to Christ, being His church. The point I am trying to bring out is that man can do and accomplish more by having a suitable help meet when he is focused on the Lord's work.

With this being said, I am not claiming men cannot dominate or accomplish without women, because they can and vice versa. As Adam was already working before the woman was formed. I am simply stating, if a husband has the right help meet, she can increase his productivity. If the woman properly aids her husband, she ultimately increases his worth and output. To find a wife is to find a good thing, and this good thing is worth it, as I will discuss in detail later in this chapter.

Before my marriage, I had big ideas about how to go about achieving my goals, businesses, books, etc. I had so many things in place that I desired to complete and fulfill. However, the real problem I had was how to implement those ideas. And honestly, I could not achieve all those things by myself; better yet have ideas and strategies of how to obtain them. I am glad to say, when my wife entered my life, she brought many strategies into the fold, whereas when I was single, I would have been sporadic with them.

I can honestly say she helped me plan and coordinate many of my book events, and she is constantly backing me up with what direction I wanted to take the family's future. She became my natural aid and support. I have accomplished more with her in the past six years than I did in the last twenty by myself, career-wise, and in internal growth.

So, husbands, although you have the potential to dominate alone, this does not mean you should. Husbands must allow their wives to aid them by keeping them close and allowing them to rejoin them. Pushing them away only decreases your productivity and self-worth. God saw a need for the wife within the relationship, so who is the husband to say the wife is useless? If anything, he should be encouraging her. It is natural for the wife to care, consider, and aid her husband. If she offers a suggestion, you should listen. And if she does not, you should ask for her opinion.

Now, back to the Lord presenting the woman to the man. When Adam laid eyes on Eve, he did not compare her to the beasts of the field or fowls of the air. He said, *"This is now bone* (strength), *of my bones* (strength), *and Flesh of my flesh."*[11] Immediately, the scripture describes how a man must leave that which he is familiar with to be with his aid. Men must learn not to compare their wives to any other person. She is not your mother, sister, cousin, or ex-girlfriend. No, she is your WIFE! She is your bone! She is your flesh!

Comparing her to another devalues her as your wife, it devalues the relationship, and it devalues how instrumental she can be in the man's life! **Proverbs 18:22** reads, *"Whoso findeth a wife findeth a good thing, and obtaineth* [12] *favor*[13] *of the*

---

[11] see **Genesis 2:23**

[12] lit. secure see Strgs#6329

[13] lit. delight see Strgs#6329

Lord."

"Good" is defined as well, beautiful, cheerful, better, pleasant, sweet, prosperity, ready, and wealth.[14] He who acquires a wife secures sweetness in his life, he acquires beauty in her and himself, he acquires prosperity and wealth, as she helps tend to the fields of his life. But before any of this can come into fruition, he must recognize her as the woman and be the only Eve in his life. No comparison period![15]

Men must be willing to give up all for their aid/help meet, leaving father, mother, the beast of the field, and all that he is familiar with to call out to his Eve by name. For she is there to provide additional strength, worth, protection, and cheerfulness when he is lacking.

The word "leave" in **Genesis 2:24** is defined as to loosen and relinquish.[16] When men see their help meet, they must relinquish and loosen any bonds that kept them tied to their kindred. The moment the man sees the woman and takes her as his wife, other interfering bonds must go. Prior relationships with other women must go. The bond of hanging out with the fellas to bowl, watch the games, etc., must go. The bond between husband and wife should not be affected by the relationship of other kinsmen.

This does not mean husbands cannot fellowship with other brethren. Or that the wife cannot find time to meet with other sisters of the body. However, I must emphasize that other obligations should not trump the bond of marriage. Men are

---

[14] see Strgs#2896

[15] The same applies to the wife, and she should not be comparing her husband to others.

[16] see Strgs#5800

charged to love their wives and to give themselves to and for her as Christ gave himself for the church, according to **Ephesians 5:25** and **Colossians 3:19**.

"Gave" in **Ephesians 5:25** is the Greek word *paradidomi* (par-ad-id'-o-mee), meaning to surrender, yield up, in trust, and transmit.[17] This is a task for us men to give ourselves over for our wives. Giving up distractions and surrendering to the love of the wife. To become one body, one spirit, which is the meaning of flesh of my flesh and bones of my bones.

Matthew 19:5 reads, *"...For this cause shall a man leave father and mother, and shall cleave to his wife: and they twain shall be one flesh?"*

Jesus, our Lord, said, it is for this reason a man leaves his father and mother, not for this reason a woman leaves her father and mother. The husband must leave, and in the process of leaving, he must join to his wife so they can become one. A man must learn to treat his wife as he would treat himself. Let me repeat myself, I say a <u>man</u> should treat his wife better than he treats his flesh.

Being the go-get-it-type of man that I am, I struggled with this very much during the early years of our marriage, and even now, I have to make efforts to put my wife first. Let me explain; I am the type of husband who likes to get things done around the house, meaning I would stay up late hours of the night building a deck, putting the kitchen together, or installing brakes on the truck. The point is, I like to get tasks completed, and this does not always make my wife happy, although she wants those things completed as well. I must also keep in mind that she also needs my time. I must not give all my time to

---

[17] see Strgs#3860

9

tending the field. I must not always be distracted; I must see my Eve and recognize her as my help meet and call her by name.

Husbands must not call their wives any other name than what they are, no slandering, no cursing, and no degradation. Why, because the husband is supposed to define his wife. He gives his wife clarity and purpose with his words. Adam defined Eve by stating, *"...she shall be called Woman, because she was taken out of Man."*[18] Woman was taken out of man; therefore, I call her woman. Adam said, I call her woman because she was created from the strength that is within man. Is this not defining?

The word "called" is the Hebrew word *qara* (kaw-raw), meaning the idea of accosting a person met, to call out to (that is to properly address by name.[19]

Husbands, I implore you to properly call out to your wife, to define your wife with words of power, purpose, and passion. Tell her that she is beautiful, shower her with words that could be used to describe the beauty of God's marvelous creation. Help her to recognize, define, and understand her talents within the garden of your life.

The moment the man begins to place others or things before his help meet is the very moment trouble will begin to arise in the relationship. However, at the same time, man's relationship with his wife should not alter or come before man's relationship with God. If anything, the wife should aid and encourage the husband's relationship with the Father. The closer the man is to God, the more loving he will become to his wife. And although the husband may be giving up all for his wife, the wife should not abuse this within her husband. There must be a balance

---

[18] See **Genesis 2:23**

[19] see Strgs#7121

between the two. If there is no balance, it would only lead to contention between the two parties.

Watchman of the Garden

Genesis 2:7 KJV:

7. And the Lord God formed man out of the dust of the ground, and breathed into his nostrils the breath of life; and man became a living soul.

Genesis 2:15 KJV:

15. And the Lord God took the man, and put him into the garden of Eden to dress it and to keep it.

In this chapter, I will be discussing the fact that man was appointed to work in the garden. Adam was created and then had to serve and worship in the garden. For a better understanding of this principle, let us define a few words seen in Genesis 2:15. These words are:

- put = to deposit by implication to allow to stay.[20]
- dress = to work, serve, and worship.[21]
- keep = to hedge about, to protect, attend to, watch, and observe.[22]

Since the beginning, it was man's job to maintain the very place where God's voice walked.[23] Falling had nothing to do with Adam needing to work. What did change after Adam's fall was the fact that Adam now had to work to produce food to sustain his natural body, for the scripture reads, *"...you will eat the herb of the field; in the sweat of your face will you eat bread..."* [24]

From these definitions, we can see and understand God's intent for man. We come to know that man was a vessel of worship, to worship in God's presence, and man was appointed to protect and observe all that took place within the garden.

To make this relevant by today's standards or view, this may be interpreted to mean it is the man's job and responsibility to protect his family by hedging them about by worshipping the Lord and having a consistent prayer life. Men maintain their families by maintaining their relationship with the Father. The husband must learn to be observant, noticing when things are not going well within the family. The husband is responsible for taking action when he sees the serpent attempting to beguile his wife. Men cannot be vigilant if they do not watch and observe. **Ezekiel 3:17** reads, *"Son of man, I have made thee a watchman*

---

[20] see Strgs#3240

[21] see Strgs#5647

[22] see Strgs#8104

[23] compare **Genesis 3:8**

[24] see **Genesis 3:17-18**

unto the house of Israel: therefore hear the word of my mouth, and give them warning from me."

Man is the Hebrew word *adam* (aw-dawm), meaning a human being, mankind, ruddy.[25] From this Hebrew word, you can see Adam's name. Therefore, when the scripture says "Son of man," it is referring to all men or even mankind at large, but for this book's purpose, we will use it as a means to refer to men.

Watchman is the Hebrew word *tsâphâh*, meaning to lean forward to peer into the distance.[26] In other words, the husband, the Adam, must watch over his household by peering into the distance through prayer so that he can be alerted to any dangers to the garden and his home. If the husband lacks in his prayer life, he is ultimately blinding his household to dangers that may exist. Let us see how **Ezekiel 33:2-7** takes this concept even further.

Ezekiel 33:2-7 KJV:

2. Son of man, speak to the children of thy people, and say unto them, when I bring the sword upon a land, if the people of the land take a man of their coasts, and set him for their watchman. **3.** If when he seeth the sword come upon the land, he blow the trumpet, and warn the people; **4.** Then whosoever heareth the sound of the trumpet and taketh not warning; if the sword come, and take him away, his blood shall be upon his own head. **5.** He heard the sound of the trumpet, and took no warning; his blood shall be upon him. But he that taketh the warning shall deliver his soul. **6.** But if the watchman sees the sword

---

[25] see Strgs#120

[26] see Strgs#6822

come, and blow not the trumpet, and the people be not warned, if the sword come, and take any person from among them, he is taken away in his iniquity; but his blood will I require at the watchman's hand. 7. So thou, O son of man, I have set thee a watchman unto the house of Israel; therefore thou shalt hear the word of my mouth, and warn them from me.

The husband, being the watchman of the house, being he was appointed to "keep," which we have learned means to watch, the husband must be vigilant of what tries to inhabit his garden. He must attend to and watch over his wife, children, and marriage. It was for this reason that the man was deposited in the garden in the first place.

I can recall times when my wife was praying intensely for herself regarding healing, decision-making, or our son. She would be praying and asking God for a breakthrough. During these times, I would be either watching television, writing, or busy with household maintenance. During these moments, she would ask me to either join her in prayer or pray for her.

Of course, being a man, I would be thinking, RIGHT NOW! Can it wait until I finish watching this, or after I paint this room? No matter how I was feeling or thinking. I always gave in to her request for prayer. And after praying, she had an answer or felt better. It's not that God did not answer her or that she has no authority. It's because the husband sets the tone for the house, and he is responsible for clearing away spiritual obstacles that attempt to hinder the wife's prayer. Just as Christ is the bridegroom and He cleared the way for the church, which is His bride.

Daniel 10:12-20 goes on by describing how an angel was charged with delivering a message to Daniel to let him know

God had heard his prayers. On his way to Daniel, the angel was held up by the Prince of the Kingdom of Persia. And the angel wrestled with the Prince of Persia for twenty-one days. The angel was not released until Michael the archangel came and helped.

So, when the wife's prayers seemed to be held up, it may take the husband's strength to free them. **1 Cor. 11:3** reads, *"But I have you know that the head of every man is Christ; and the head of the woman is the man; and the head of Christ is God."*

Therefore, what the wife feels is important, and the husband should keep himself available for her. He should be willing to hear out her emotions and concerns, and not be so quick to push aside what she is feeling as being too emotional.

The man/husband must put away what distracts him from his duty of being the watchman and protector of the house. The husband must know when to step in and end both natural and spiritual situations. He is the protector of God's dwelling place. Ultimately, his actions alter the course of the household, doing all the necessary things to keep the house (garden) in order. That includes, and is not limited to, bringing roses, jewelry, and chocolates to make his wife happy.

The husband often has to step out of himself to satisfy his other self (his wife). And to be honest, the man is responsible for taking up the mantle of worship in the household, as man was the first to be ordered by God to the practice of worship. His worship and prayers limit and hinder the serpent's ability to dwell and mislead.[27]

The lioness (wife) may be a fierce hunter and but the lion (husband) sets the boundary of the Kingdom. In other words,

---

[27] compare **Genesis 2:15** - dress = worship

the wife may pray for the family and love, as she enters the spiritual battlefield, yet it takes the husband's worship and prayer to establish the work.

Obey The Voice

Genesis 2:15-17 KJV:

15. And the Lord God took man, and put him into the garden of Eden to dress it and to keep it. **16**. And the Lord God commanded the man, saying, of every tree of the garden thou mayest freely eat: **17**. But of the tree of the knowledge of good and evil, thou shalt not eat of it: for the day that thou eatest thereof thou shalt surely die.

Lastly, the man must not take heed to what his wife says over what God has commanded him directly. Although a man must give up all for his wife, the words she speaks must not interfere with or trump the instructions he received from God. It is his responsibility to maintain the area in which God walks. The husband must understand his walk with God to balance his walk with his wife, as long as the two remain in the same garden of God.

"Command" in **Genesis 2:16** is the Hebrew word *tsavah*

(tsaw-vaw), meaning to constitute, enjoin, appoint, forbid, send a messenger, and set in order.[28] Regarding the Tree of the Knowledge of Good and Evil, the Lord forbade Adam to eat of it, while simultaneously appointing Adam to be the messenger for that same commandment. It became Adam's job to relay God's command to later people.

In other words, it is the husband's job to minister to his wife after hearing the commands of the Lord, for he has been appointed by God as a messenger. Both husband and wife must be on one accord, and they must stand on one command, the word of the Lord. If the husband and wife cannot agree or come to a conclusion regarding a decision, they must then stand on the word of the Lord for an answer.

When the commandment is not shared properly, and both parties are acting on their own will, it leaves the potential for what God said to be twisted. And the result of a twisted message may cause those who hear it to fall. **Matthew 12:25** states, *"And Jesus knew their thoughts, and said unto them, Every kingdom divided against itself is brought to desolation*[29]*; and every city or house divided against itself shall not stand."*

Now compare **Matthew 12:25** with **Mark 4:13-15**, *"And he said unto them, know ye not this parable? And how then will ye know all parables? The sower soweth the word. And these are they by the way side, where the word is sown; but when they have heard, Satan cometh immediately*[30] *and taketh away the word that was sown in their hearts."*

Divided in **Matthew 12:25** is defined as apportion, share, to

---

[28] see Strgs#6680

[29] lit. lay waste

[30] immediately = directly, at once or soon Strgs#2112

disunite, differ, deal, be different between, distribute[31]. And "take away" in **Mark 4:15** is defined as to lift, take up or away, to keep in suspense within the mind, make to doubt[32]. Oxford Dictionary defines suspense as *a state or feeling of excited or anxious uncertainty about what may happen.*

In other words, if the husband does not deliver the message as God intended or if the wife does not hear correctly from the husband, it can cause division between the two. This mishearing not only causes division, but the scripture states Satan has the potential to come and take the word which was spoken, causing one to doubt what God said by keeping them in suspense within their mind.

Husbands must relay the Lord's command and adhere to it; they must not allow the enemy to bring about disunity within their marriage by division or mishearing. Disunity within a marriage will only cause it not to stand. The words "not stand" come from two Greek words, "not," being defined as never, neither, and unworthy. The second is "stand," which is defined as to abide. In essence, disunity causes a house/marriage to become unworthy to abide in. As long as the husband and wife allow division to come between them, the harder it will be for them to abide by their covenant.

I cannot emphasize enough how important it is for the husband to be a messenger of God within his household. He must deliver a sure word to his wife and family so the word does not become stolen by the enemy and then used against them. **Genesis 3:1-7** clearly illustrates what happens when husband and wife doubt and mishear the word of God in their

---

[31] see Strgs#3307

[32] see Strgs#142

union.

Genesis 3:1-7 KJV:

1. Now the serpent was more subtil than any beast of the field which the Lord God had made. And he said unto the woman, Yea, hath God said, Ye shall not eat of every tree of the garden?
2. And the woman said unto the serpent, We may eat of the fruit of the trees of the garden.
3. But of the fruit of the tree which is in the midst of the garden, God hath said, Ye shall not eat of it, neither shall ye touch it, lest ye die.
4. And the serpent said unto the woman, Ye shall not surely die.
5. For God doth know that in the day ye eat thereof, then your eyes shall be opened, and ye shall be as gods, knowing good and evil.
6. And the woman saw that the tree was good for food, and that it was pleasant to the eyes, and a tree to be desired to make one wife, she took of the fruit thereof, and did eat, and gave also unto her husband with her; and he did eat.
7. And the eyes of them both were opened, and they knew that they were naked; and they sewed fig leaves together, and made themselves aprons.

When we look at the interaction between Adam, Eve, and the serpent, there is a lot we can take from it when considering mistakes within marriage. The first mistake made within the conversation is the fact that Eve allowed the serpent to twist the command of God, which caused her to doubt the commands

God had given. God never told them they could not touch the fruit, but that they could not eat of it. Having the commands of God stolen by the enemy was one of the very reasons Eve then considered the words of the serpent.

The word "saw" in **Genesis 3:6** is defined as to consider, behold, and take heed. By having what was spoken stolen from her, she no longer had the commands of the Lord to stand on when being challenged, which then put her in the terrible position of considering the words of the serpent to eat the fruit.

The second and most important thing we can learn from the interaction is the fact that Adam failed to do his job. Adam should have stepped in and reconfirmed the commands of the Lord over his wife once he heard her misspeak them. He should have also put the serpent in its place, being that he was appointed the protector and keeper of the garden. This is all part of protecting the commandments of the Lord, which he shared with his wife. Adam's job was to protect and uphold the commandments of the Lord in the Garden. By upholding the commands, the word of the Lord would continue to land on the good ground of her heart.

Jesus stated, *"Thou shalt love the Lord thy God with all thy heart, and with all thy soul, and with all thy mind. This is the first and great commandment*[33]*."* It is important that the husband always take the commands of the Lord over whatever else is being spoken, whether they be his thoughts, words of the serpent, or from his wife. The husband helps to establish God's commands by being the proper messenger of God within the marriage and household.

---

[33] see **Matthew 22:37-38**

Protecting His Heart

Now that I have covered the husband's role within the marriage, I will discuss a biblical view of the wife's role.

Genesis 2:20-22 KJV:

20. And Adam gave names to all the cattle, and to the fowl of the air, and to every beast of the field; but for Adam there was not found an help meet for him. **21.** And the Lord God caused a deep sleep to fall upon Adam, and he slept: and he took one of his ribs, and closed up the flesh instead thereof; **22.** And the rib, which the Lord God had taken from man, made he woman, and brought her unto the man.

As stated in verse twenty of the above passage, Adam did not find a help meet among the beasts of the field or fowl of the air. The phrase "not found" is defined as to appear, exist, to attain, acquire, or be present[34]. We have read, there was no help meet present among those things which were created, and because of this, the Lord continued to create, first by putting Adam to sleep and then by taking away a rib. From that rib, God would create the proper help meet for man.

Again, according to the passage above, the woman would be created as a help meet for man. One of the definitions for the word "taken" in verse twenty-two comes from the Hebrew word *laqach* (law-kakh), meaning reserve[35]. In other words, the woman was reserved for a man; she was always part of the plan. To prove this further, in **Genesis 1:26** God said, *"Let us make man in our image."* The word "man" used here in Genesis 1:26 is defined as mankind and species[36]. In His creation of man, God saw in Adam, the human species, both man and woman, because the woman was reserved within man. In **Judges 21:22,** it talks about the women from Shiloh not being reserved for each man from the war. The word reserved in **Judges 21:22** is the same Hebrew laqach for taken used in **Genesis 2:22**.

The woman was always meant to be the help meet of man, not an animal and not another man. The woman is the opposite of the man, making her perfect for aiding him. help meet is the Hebrew word *'ezer*, meaning aid[37]. It comes from the Hebrew root word *azar*, meaning to surround and protect[38].

Ezer consists of the Hebrew pictographic letters, *ayin, zayin,* and *reysh*. Like many other ancient cultures, such as the

---

[34] see Strgs#4672

[35] see Strgs#3947

[36] see Strgs#120

[37] see Strgs#5828

[38] see Strgs#5826

Egyptians, each letter consisted of a picture, and with each picture came a meaning. Therefore, *ayin* is the picture of an eye and means to see or experience. *Zayin* is the picture of a weapon and means to cut or to cut off. Finally, there is *reyesh,* which is the picture of a head, and it means a person. If we were to read these pictures as a sentence, it could be interpreted to say, to experience the person with the weapon. This person with the weapon would be the woman of protection.

In the eyes of the Lord, the woman was purposely created to help surround and protect the man. The woman is not haphazard or a second thought. The man did not fail when it came to choosing the woman, he chose correctly. *"THIS IS NOW BONES OF MY BONES AND FLESH OF MY FLESH!"* Adam not only chose correctly, but he was also apparently excited when he chose.

The word "now" is defined as to stroke, beat, anvil, to say with repetition.[39] I can only imagine the pride and happiness Adam had when he laid eyes upon the first woman, the mother of the human species, crafted directly by the hands of God. I can see him being excited, beating his puffed-up chest, chanting, "This is now bones of my bones and flesh of my flesh!"

Women, if your husband or potential half is not excited and beating his chest when he sees you, or if he focuses more on himself than on you, I would question his loyalty and love. Ladies, you are wonderfully made, crafted by the very hands of God. Women should never accept the words of any man if they do not respect their position as a wonderful creation. If he is not respecting your beauty, then he is not of God, the scripture

---

[39] see Strgs#6471

states, "He has made everything beautiful in its time."[40] If he does not respect your beauty, then he does not respect God, and thus he cannot be of God.

Diane Sumler explained it this way in her book *Divine Direction*:

"It is not the job of the woman to find a husband! Instead, she must be found in the Lord, as it was God who "brought" her to Adam. Ladies must understand that their Adam must first come to the realization that God must create a wife for him because what exists/what he has experienced is not comparable. If a man has not yet realized this, then he is not ready for a wife."

Once chosen, the woman/wife role is to protect her husband. You may be asking how the wife surrounds and protects her husband when he is the protector of the garden/household. Well, wives protect their husbands through the act of speaking good over their name through prayer and in public.

1 Peter 3:1-6 KJV:

1. Likewise, ye wives, be in subjection to your own husband; that, if any obey not the words, they also may without the word be won by the conversation of the wives;
2. While they behold your chaste conversation coupled with fear.
3. Whose adorning let it not be that outward adorning of plaiting the hair, and of wearing of gold, or of putting on apparel;

---

[40] see **Eccl. 3:11**

4. But let it be the hidden man of the heart, in that which is not corruptible, even the ornament of a meek and quiet spirit, which is in the sight of God of great price.

5. For after this manner in the old time the holy women also, who trusted in God, adorned themselves, being in subjection unto their own husbands:

6. Even as Sarah obeyed Abraham, calling him lord: whose daughters ye are, as long as ye do well and are not afraid of any amazement.

According to Peter the Apostle, wives must keep a chaste conversation. Chaste is defined as clean, innocent, modest, and perfect.[41] Wives must have and keep a clean conversation[42] when it concerns their husbands and household.

In verse six of **1 Peter 3**, it states that Sarah obeyed Abraham and called him lord. When wives are discussing their husbands, it is important, they respect and honor their name. In other words, wives must speak highly of their husbands and not tear down their name through vile conversation. **Proverbs 31:10-31** goes on to state that a virtuous woman's husband has trust in her, wisdom, and the law of kindness is in her mouth.

The wife must not belittle or tear down their husband's name when talking to their friend and family. The wife must honor him by submitting to his title of being her husband. If the wife does not honor him, his name, and his title, she will struggle with submission to him. And if there is a problem with submission, there will always be contention within the union. The husband will surrender his heart and trust in her

---

[41] see Strgs#53

[42] lit. behavior Strgs#391

when he knows and understands his heart will be protected by her using the weapon of God's word.

Not receiving the respect of his wife, the husband is unlikely to do his duty of giving up all for her, and will struggle with loving her. This is proven by Paul commanding men to love their wives.[43] Men long for a sense of respect. I am not saying that women do not want respect, but it is a part of men's nature to have it. It is evident throughout the scripture that women have the need to feel love, while men desire respect. Christ, the husband, is revered and worshipped, while we, the church/his bride, desire to be loved by him.

Secondly, the wife must protect her husband by being his watchman. To better understand this, we will read **Matthew 26:40-41** and **Matthew 24:43**.

Matthew 26:40-41 KJV:

40. And he cometh unto the disciples, and findeth them asleep, and saith unto Peter, What, could ye not watch with me one hour? **41.** Watch and pray, that ye enter not into temptation: the spirit indeed is willing, but the flesh is weak.

Matthew 24:43 KJV:

43. But know this, that if the goodman of the house had known in what watch the thief would come, he would have watched, and would not have suffered his house to be broken up.

In both verses above, the Lord said to watch and pray; doing

---

[43] see **Col. 3:19**

so keeps your house from being broken up and keeps us from entering into temptation. The "first watch" in **Matthew 24:43** is defined as guarding, to keep an eye upon, to guard a person by protecting them from another person or thing.

And as stated previously, "help meet" means to surround and protect, so a way the wife protects her husband is through prayer. It is important the wife covers her husband, not only in prayer, but also with good words. Her prayers help to keep him from temptation and protect him from being attacked by both spiritual and physical elements. The very words she speaks hedge him about.

Psalms 128:3 states, *"Thy wife shall be as a fruitful vine by the sides of thine house."* Vine is defined as to bend (as twining). Sides are defined as the flanks.[44] In other words, like a vine, the wife is responsible for surrounding or wrapping the house in and with fruitfulness. When the husband is out working and protecting the garden, the wife should be covering him and the house with fruitful words. Words that will strengthen and encourage him to remain in the work. Without her support, he may struggle to remain because she is an additional strength for him, as she was made from his bone to be his help meet.

---

[44] see Strgs#1612 and 3411

No Other Instructions

Chapter five is very similar to the chapter *Obey the Voice*, in that many must obey the voice of God at all times. Here, this chapter will dive into the idea of how the wife must not give contradicting instructions to her husband after God has already instructed him on a matter. As explained in previous chapters, women were created and reserved to aid men with his work. With a woman at his side, a man is capable of accomplishing more than he could alone. The woman should and is there to build up the man, supporting him with his task, a task that should be God-centered.

The woman came from man, and thus, she is the perfect being to aid him. Knowing this, the woman must do her best to protect the heart of a man, as described in the previous chapter. Man was commanded to give up all for the woman, now having the heart of man, the woman/wife must protect it just as the man protects and keeps the garden.

If the woman does not keep in mind the duties of the man and does not hold his best interest. She can bring about his ruin if her words and suggestions are the opposite of what God said. When a man truly gives up all for his wife, he is literally placing his heart in her hands. Having his heart, the woman/wife must be careful of how she handles it. To better understand this point, let us read **Genesis 3:1-6**.

Genesis 3:1-6 KJV:

1. Now the serpent was more subtil than any beast of the field which the Lord God had made. And he said unto the woman, Yea, hath God said, Ye shall not eat of every tree of the garden?
2. And the woman said unto the serpent, We may eat of the fruit of the trees of the garden.
3. But of the fruit of the tree which is in the midst of the garden, God hath said, Ye shall not eat of it, neither shall ye touch it, lest ye die.
4. And the serpent said unto the woman, Ye shall not surely die!
5. For God doth know that in the day ye eat thereof, then your eyes shall be opened, and ye shall be as gods, knowing good and evil.
6. And when the woman saw that the tree was good for food, and that it was pleasant to the eyes, and a tree to be desired to make me wise, she took of the fruit thereof, and did eat, and gave also unto her husband with her; and he did eat.

The word "saw" in verse six is defined as advise self, enjoy, have experience, gaze, take heed, and consider.[45] The word

---

[45] see Strgs#7200

"pleasant" is defined as a longing, delight, satisfaction, dainty, charm.[46] We read here that Eve saw (lit. gave self-advice) that the fruit was pleasant (delightful) to eat. In essence, she took her eyes off aiding the man with the garden and took on her pleasures.

Eve was educated on what God had said regarding the tree of good and evil, for Adam must have instructed her on the matter. Adam had to instruct her on God's clear instruction because when God told Adam not to eat of the tree of the knowledge of Good and Evil, Eve had not yet been created (see **Genesis 2:1-17**). It was not until after God's instruction not to eat from the tree that woman was created (see **Genesis 2:18**). So, Adam must have done his duty of instructing Eve on the commandments of God.

Knowing the instruction of the Lord, Eve still gave in to what she desired and gave to her husband, who was with her. And after he ate, sin was committed. Although the man gives up all for the woman, the woman cannot and should not make her desire his. The man had instructions from God. It is when the man disobeys and becomes sidetracked from God's direction that things go wrong.

In **Genesis 3:6-7**, it was not until Adam ate of the fruit that their eyes were opened. **Romans 5:12** states, *"by one man's sin, death entered the world."* Not by one man and woman's sin, but one man, Adam. Women possess enough influence in a relationship that they can sway and have power over a man's heart, which could be used to cause him to question God's instruction and bring about death to their existence.

A wife must take caution in how she speaks to the man, along

---

[46] see Strgs#8378

with how she acts towards her husband. Her words can either bring them closer or drive them apart. Both Eve's words and actions help to drive the wedge of death into their spiritual relationship, with each other and with God. This was also witnessed in the life of Abraham and Sarah, then Abram and Sarai.

God promised Abram a seed, and from that seed, many nations would spring up. However, we learned in **Genesis 15** and **16**, when Sarai did not bear a child in their time, that Sarai urged Abram to have a child by one of her handmaids named Hagar. The scripture states Abram *"hearkened to the voice of Sarai."* Hearkened is the Hebrew word *"shama"*; shaw-mah, meaning to hear intelligently (often with the implication of attention and obedience)[47].

Abram took obedience to the voice of Sarai, allowing her command to override the very words the Lord had spoken to him. Similar to Adam, God instructed Abram not his wife, and also like Adam and Eve, by the man listening to the voice and command of his wife over the Lord, their relationship was affected. Because of both Abram and Sarai's disobedience, a woman and child were exiled from them, to eventually become a nation that would oppose the promised seed.

Also, like Adam and Eve, the blame cannot be solely on the woman. Her eating the fruit or speaking those words did not upset their balance in the garden, but the actions of Adam did. The scripture clearly states that Eve gave to her husband, who was with her. It does not state that Adam came to her after the serpent finished talking with her or that she took it to him afterward.

---

[47] see Strgs#8085

No, she gave it to her husband, who was with her. This places the blame on Adam as well; he knew God's instruction more than Eve, as he received it firsthand. Adam should have protected his wife from the subtle words of the serpent because he was given charge to dress, keep, and protect the garden.

However, I said all this to emphasize how the wife must know how to handle the heart of man, by not presenting that which would hinder his relationship with her and God. He will eat from the fruit of her words when presented to him, good and bad. She must not speak words that would make him unfit to protect the garden (their home).

Jesus said, *"A good man out of the good treasure of his heart bringeth forth that which is good; and an evil man out of the evil treasure of his heart bringeth forth that which is evil: for of the abundance of the heart his mouth speakers"*[48] "Treasure" is the Greek word *thesauros*, which is a deposit or wealth of words. Wives must speak wisely to their husbands, lest they take the bad treasure and eat. My wife often told me later in our marriage, "Sometimes being your wife, I had to learn not to tell you what to do, even if I knew the outcome. I had to let you make decisions on your own, whether good or bad, so that you would learn how to be a man."

This is especially true when disagreements come, and they will, no matter how holy we are. When disagreement occurs, both parties must learn not to speak words that would alter the performance of the other, even if one party knows the truth. Sometimes we must allow emotions to play out, yet as they play out, words must be used cautiously.

The wife must not offer her husband fruits of anger, bitter-

---

[48] see **Luke 6:45**

ness, hate, or jealousy. She must offer and speak encouraging, loving, and respectful words to her husband. Doing so will allow him to work and tend to the garden of their home as the Lord intended.

Birthing A Thing

Genesis 1:26-28 KJV:

26. And God said, let us make man in our image, after our likeness: and let them have dominion over the fish of the sea, and over the fowl of the air, and over the cattle and over all the earth, and over every creeping thing that creepeth upon the earth. **27.** So, God created man in his image, in the image of God created he him, male and female created he them. **28.** And God blessed them, and God said unto them, Be fruitful, and multiply, and replenish the earth, and subdue it: and have dominion over the fish of the sea, and over the fowl of the air, and over every living thing that moveth upon the earth.

Genesis 5:4 NASB:

4. Then the days of Adam after he became the father of Seth were eight hundred years, and he had other sons and daughters.

The final thought I would like to bring out concerning the place of the wife is the idea of how the wife is there to bring forth or birth new things into the family. This birthing can be that of natural children or of simply giving the husband new ideas of what direction the family should go.

Being a wife does not mean the wife is useless or that she must sit in the house powerless. No, just like a lioness, the wife rules and reigns in her own house. She controls the so-called ins and outs, while the husband (the lion) establishes the house. Although the lioness is subordinate to the lion, it is the lioness who is known for being a strong and fierce hunter. The husband does not make the house alone, it is the wife who brings value and adds to the house.

Psalms 128:3 reads, *"Thy wife shall be as a fruitful vine by the sides of thine house."* "Fruitful" is defined as to bear fruit, to make fruitful, to branch off.[49]

Psalms 105:24 reads, *"And he (Jacob) increased his people greatly, and made them stronger than their enemies."* The word increase in Psalms 105:24 is the same Hebrew word used for fruitful in **Psalms 128:3**. Vine is the Hebrew word *gephen*, gheh-fen, meaning to bend, a vine (as twining), and a vine of prosperity.[50]

By the sides translates as flank or recess.[51] However, it originates from the Hebrew root word *yarek*, yaw-rake; meaning thigh, generative parts, loins (as the seat of procreative power), and outside of the thigh (where the sword was worn)[52].

---

[49] see Strgs#6509

[50] see Strgs#1612

[51] see Strgs#3411

[52] see Strgs#3409

Finally, "house" is defined as family.[53] In other words, the wife shall be an increasing vine of prosperity that supports the word of God in thy family. She is also there to support and cushion the procreative power of the man. The man is the sword, and the wife is the sheath. Women were made with the type of love that allows them to endure all that men may come up with or do. A good wife can and should support her man through all trials, as long as she remains at his side, she adds value to him.

And the very words she speaks or the actions she takes can cause him to follow new dreams and goals. A biblical wife must carry love, comfort, and support within her being. During my early years of marriage, I often made and even now make wrong decisions for the family. Yet my wife supported me through it all. She could have cursed and blamed me for all of it. However, she remained a godly wife, upholding the sword of God's word in the house, along with the direction I desired to take the family.

A wife must not view the husband's mistakes as failures, but appreciate the direction he desires to lead the family. She supports, comforts, brings forth, and increases her husband. And just like the wife that was written about in previous changes, the husband must not abuse this within her, and if he gives up all for her, he will know not to do this.

The modern marriage between husband and wife must change. The husband must view his wife as being valuable and not that of being a lower thing, for she is his worth. Secondly, the wife must not fight to establish herself in the house, she must know that she is a fierce lioness ordained by God within the house. She is the vine that increases prosperity, yet holds

---

[53] see Strgs#1004

and binds the household together by supporting the sword.

Neither husband nor wife should be fighting for dominance over the house. Paul, the apostle, wrote it plainly, *"Wives, submit yourselves unto your own husbands, as unto the Lord.... Husbands, love your wives, even as Christ also loved the church, and gave himself for it."*[54] If the wife submits and the husband loves, there would be no need to battle. No contention, only love, for God is ultimately the head of all.[55]

So, wives know you are valuable in the house! Know you are a mighty supporter of the word! And know your actions and words have the potential to stir up prosperity within your husband! No, your very support can help birth a thing in your husband, in your children, and within yourself.

---

[54] see **Eph. 5:22 & 25**

[55] see **1 Cor. 11:3**

A Woman's Prepared Glory

There are many single women in the world who are believers and who are seeking a husband. It took me a long time to be able to understand the process of courting, dating, and desiring a spouse. I understand women's desire to have a husband, and many have tried various techniques to search for their possible spouse.

Some of them have been successful and others, not so much. For those who have not had success with coming into contact with their future spouse, I hope the information I share in this chapter will not only be encouraging to you but also helpful with this particular journey of your life.

I believe many single women go about seeking out their future husband the wrong way, by using techniques shared by the world. And when these techniques fail, they become discouraged at the idea of never being married. So, in this chapter, I will not be discussing a technique created by man, but a technique God established since the creation of man.

When it comes to marriage and the idea of dating, Jesus

referred back to the first union, stating, *"For this cause shall a man leave father and mother and shall cleave to his wife, and the two shall be one flesh."*[56]

Paul himself went as far as to say, *"For this cause shall a man leave his father and mother, and shall be joined unto his wife, and they two shall be one flesh. This is a great mystery: but I speak concerning Christ and the church."*[57]

With this being said, we must use the first marriage between Adam and Eve as a guideline for a proper relationship. It was mentioned in previous chapters that Eve was seen by Adam when she was brought to him in the garden, and how Adam chose her over the rest of creation. Therefore, it is important women are first seen by their potential husbands when they are both present in the garden. This brings about the questions: What does it mean to be seen, and what does it mean to be in the garden?

For this question, let us read **Genesis 2:18**, *"And the Lord God said, It is not good that the man should be alone; I will make him an help meet for him."*

From this passage, we can conclude that work happens in the garden, due to the fact that man was placed in the garden.[58] Because of the work, God decided it was good for man to have a help meet to assist with the Garden. Once Adam's help meet was created and the first woman was brought to him, Adam saw his wife for the first time.[59] Women are seen by their potential spouse when she is aiding and working to build up the same

---

[56] see **Matthew 19:5** KJV, compare **Genesis 2:24**

[57] see **Ephesians 5:32**

[58] see **Genesis 2:15**

[59] see **Genesis 2:22**

garden, he is in. If a man is in the garden working, he cannot see his potential wife if she is not being a help meet in the same garden.

What is the garden, you may ask? The garden is the Kingdom of God, and working means being active in the ministry.[60] Working in the ministry does not necessarily mean being a member of the same church. No, working in the garden describes an individual who is actively laboring to help bring lost souls to Christ. Single women must prepare themselves to be seen by working in the garden, so when the bridegroom comes, he takes notice of her, her work, and her glory.

Women must and should choose a man who is already working in the garden. It was easy for Eve to submit to Adam because he was already doing the work; her purpose of creation was to aid him. And if he was not working, she herself would not be working in the purpose for which she created.

We, the bride of Christ/the church, submit ourselves to Christ because He has shown His work for the ministry and willingness to die for His bride.

To truly understand what marriage is to look like, we have to examine the relationship between Christ and His Church. The qualities of marriage must match the qualities of how Christ treats His church. If you desire to know if your husband is treating you right, then examine how Christ treats His Church.

Let's take a step back before even approaching the idea of marriage, to examine if your potential bridegroom is treating Christ with reverence, respect, loyalty, and love? If he is not, then he is not the one for you, for a believing bridegroom can only treat you as good as he treats his God. If he loves

---

[60] compare **Eph. 4:12**

and respects our Messiah with the honor He has, then your bridegroom will bestow that same honor upon you.

As a side note, if you happened to get saved after getting married, **1 Corinthians 7:14-15** states, *"For the unbelieving husband is sanctified by the wife, and the unbelieving wife is sanctified by the husband: else were your children unclean; but now are they holy. But if the unbelieving depart, let him depart. A brother or sister is not under bondage in such cases, but God hath called us to peace."*

Yes, wives possess the gift to sanctify their husbands and children. Remember, wives wrap and protect the home. With this being said, women should not go into a marriage already unequally yoked, hoping and believing they can change their potential husband. The above passage refers to wives who become saved after being married, for **1 Corinthians 7:10** says, *"And unto the married I command"*. Now let's get back to focusing on the bride and the bridegroom.

Matthew 25:1-13 KJV:

1. Then shall the kingdom of heaven be likened unto ten virgins, which took their lamps, and went forth to meet the bridegroom.
2. And five of them were wise, and five were foolish.
3. They that were foolish took their lamps, and took no oil with them:
4. But the wise took oil in their vessels with their lamps.
5. While the bridegroom tarried, they all slumbered and slept.
6. And at midnight there was a cry made, Behold, the bridegroom cometh; go ye out to meet him.
7. Then all those virgins arose, and trimmed their lamps.

8. And the foolish said unto the wise, Give us of your oil; for our lamps are gone out.

9. But the wise answered, saying, Not so; lest there be not enough for us and you: but go ye rather to them that sell, and buy for yourselves.

10. And while they went to buy, the bridegroom came; and they that were ready went in with him to the marriage: and the door was shut.

11. Afterward came also the other virgins, saying, Lord, Lord, open to us.

12. But he answered and said, Verily I say unto you, I know you not.

13. Watch therefore, for ye know neither the day nor the hour wherein the Son of man cometh.

In the parable of the Ten Virgins, Jesus gives us a better understanding of how the virgin, the possible bride, should react when presenting herself to the bridegroom. With this being stated, let us take a look at several definitions, with the first being virgins.

"Virgin" is defined as a marriageable maiden, an unmarried daughter.[61] "Wise" is defined as thoughtful, discreet (cautious character), sagacious (having or showing keen mental discernment and good judgment), practical skill, and intelligence.[62] And lastly, the word "foolish" is defined as dull, stupid (as if shut up), heedless, (morally) a blockhead, and absurd.[63]

Therefore, these virgins were being presented as individuals

---

[61] see Strgs#3933

[62] see Strgs#5429

[63] see Strgs#3474

seeking to marry and to be chosen by the bridegroom when he arrives. When women are looking to present themselves to a potential partner, it is imperative that they be wise, making wise decisions by putting their emotions aside to examine the bridegroom thoroughly by using their intelligence, keen mental discernment, and good judgment.

To know by seeing if their bridegroom carries a title of honor, expressive respect and reverence to God, himself, and the bride. The bridegroom must carry the same light that is in the virgin or bride, to be equally yoked, and that light is Christ and the reverence for Him.

Jesus goes on and describes how there were ten virgins and how five of them were foolish by not preparing themselves to be seen by the bridegroom when he arrived. Their preparation was described as having oil and the trimming of their lamps. With this being said, once the bridegroom arrived, the five virgins who did not prepare themselves were left behind for not doing the necessary work for his arrival. They missed their opportunity to be seen, they missed their opportunity to have their light or glory be seen. Having the bridegroom say, *"Verily I say unto you, I know you not."*

The word "know" in this particular passage is the Greek word *eido*[64], which is defined as to know by seeing. To be seen by the bridegroom, the virgins had to have their lamps properly filled with oil and wicks trimmed. In other words, her life must be filled with oil of the spirit, and her life has to be prepared by doing work, which helps to intensify her glory. Lamp comes from a Greek root word meaning to radiate

---

[64] see Strgs#1492

brilliancy.[65] "Trimmed" in **Matthew 25:7** is defined as to put in proper order, make ready, and prepare.[66] Being prepared and having things in order allowed the virgins to radiate brilliantly, enabling the bridegroom to take notice and bring them into his kingdom.

If compared to Genesis chapter two, women were made to aid man in the garden; it is when women effectively work in the garden that their lamps burn brighter, putting them in a position to be seen by their bridegroom. If the bride does not have her work in proper order, her lamps of brilliancy will not be illuminated, which will cause her to be overlooked in the garden by the bridegroom.

Revelation 21:2 reads, *"And I John saw the holy city, new Jerusalem, coming down from God out of heaven, prepared as a bride adorned for her husband."* Here in **Revelation 21:2** and **Genesis 2:22**, it is God who allows the union of the bride and bridegroom. Within this pattern, the bridegroom lays his life down to have his help meet created, and the bride herself is in place and prepared to aid the bridegroom.

The word "prepared" in **Revelation 21:2** comes from the Greek word *hetoimos*, meaning to adjust.[67] Single women, if you desire to have a husband, I suggest you adjust your lifestyle by focusing on working in the Lord's Garden. Working in His garden causes the oil in you to fill and flow, for it is His oil which illuminates your presence, which allows the bride to be seen by their potential husband. God's work comes first, then your presentation to the bridegroom.

---

[65] see Strgs#2985 & 2989

[66] see Strgs#2885

[67] see Strgs#2092

This same correlation can be seen with Jesus and His church. Jesus did not marry His church until He had effectively laid His life down for her. And the church does not get to marry Him until she has worked in the garden of the earth, to help lead souls to the Father. It is after she works that Jesus comes back, sees her lanterns (her beauty and glory), and marries her. Men can only see a woman's true glory once she has prepared herself to be seen and after he has laid his life down. It is preparing and working in the garden of the ministry, which exposes the virgin's beauty.

God the Head

Matthew 22:37-38 K.J.V:

37. Jesus said unto him, Thou shalt love the Lord thy God with all thy heart, and with all thy soul, and with all thy mind. **38.** This is the first and great commandment.

1 Cor. 11:3 KJV:

3. But I would have you know, that the head of every man is Christ; and the head of woman is the man; and the head of Christ is God.

Man and woman must both have a personal relationship with God and obey His commandments. With this in mind, let's break down what the Lord declared the greatest commandment.

- all = the Greek word *holos,* meaning whole, complete,

throughout the whole.

- heart = thoughts, feelings (mind).
- soul = breath, spirit, vital force.
- mind = deep thoughts, disposition, and understanding.
- first = foremost, before, beginning, chief.
- great = big, mega, high, strong.

In essence, Christ was stating that, above all things, the very first thing humanity should worry about is loving God. And this should be the primary thing on our list: love God with our heart (thoughts and feelings), love Him with our soul (every breath and vital force), and love Him with our mind (understanding and deepest thoughts).

Loving the Father comes before husband, wife, or children. Loving Him should be chief and foremost in our lives. As a household and being part of the church, the husband and wife must learn to practice all that was mentioned in this book, plus more concerning husband and wife, but with God first.

Speaking of love, I would like to bring up another point that was made by my good friend. When teaching, she said, "Just because you are not married, doesn't mean you are second-rate in the kingdom." I believe this to be true, yes, those who are not married are not any less than those who are married. She also made the point that Genesis chapter two does say the Lord states that it is not good for man to be alone. However, one can be single and not be alone, as the Lord was always present with Adam in the Garden. Those who are single can surround themselves with friends and family, more importantly, with God.

"And I will pray the Father, and he shall give you another

Comforter, that he may abide[68] with you for ever."[69]

"Nevertheless, I tell you the truth; It is expedient for you that I go away: for if I go not away, the Comforter will not come unto you; but if I depart, I will send Him unto you."[70]

Though one may appear single or alone, this is far from the actual truth. Being a believer of Christ, our Messiah has made a promise to each of us if we believe what He has said. This truth is that He has sent the comfort of the Holy Spirit unto us, to abide, to stay, to reside with us forever. Whether single or married, the Comforter is always with us, ensuring that we are alone.

Paul himself even said, *"I say therefore to the unmarried and widows, It is good for them if they abide even as I. But if they cannot contain, let them marry: for it is better to marry than burn."[71]*

From the previous passage, we can see that Paul himself was single, and he made the point that if you are single and keeping yourself, it is a good thing. The word good is the Greek word, *kalos*, meaning beautiful, good, valuable, or virtuous (for appearance or use, and thus distinguished from what is properly intrinsic).[72]

If one is single and if one is exercising self-restraint in their body for the work of the Lord, it is a good and beautiful thing. Why, because one who is single can devote themselves to the Lord. And to devote yourself to Christ does not mean a single person has to live and work at the church more than any other

---

[68] abide = to stay. see Strgs#3306

[69] see **John 14:16**

[70] see **John 16:7**

[71] see **1 Corinthians 7:8-9**

[72] see Strgs#2570

person. For we are all called to be holy priests [73], the single are not the only ones who must be devout.

To devote one's life to Christ means to love God and to love your neighbors. God is for both the married and the single. However, those who are single are not distracted by the aspect of marriage and can freely give themselves to Christ.

Those who are single, do not become discouraged or believe that you have to be married. For God is the Head of all who believe, married and single. If you are single, you carry the same value as those who are not. Paul was single, Mary Magdalena was single, and they both did amazing things in the Lord.

We must be willing to give up distractions (see **Eph. 4:22-32**), we must be a Watchmen in God's garden while working in his ministry (see **Isaiah 21:6-8**), obey the voice of the Lord (see **Deut. 8:18-20**), protect the heart or defend our belief (see **1 Peter 3:15**), hear no other instructions (see **Hebrews 11:8**), and birth a thing (see **Gal. 4:19**). We must do this, for Christ is the bridegroom, and we look to serve and worship Him.

We illustrate to the Father we love Him when we open our thoughts and feelings to Him. When He becomes our vital force or breath of life[74], and when we understand that He must come first in all things. He should be mega in our lives, and this is primary in all we do. He desires to have the whole of us. God wants the household. He wants the church to be both protectors of the garden and the bride.

---

[73] compare **1 Peter 2:5**

[74] compare **Genesis 2:23**

HER

Mentorship in Marriage

I always wanted to be married and have a family of my own. I had some sense of how things should be in a marriage, but had not necessarily seen much of it in action. But as the scriptures say, "If thou knowest not, thou shalt asketh somebody." All jokes aside, this is what the scripture says in **Titus 2:1-5**, "*1. But speak thou the things which become sound doctrine: 2. That the aged men be sober, grave, temperate, sound in faith, in charity, in patience. 3. The aged women likewise, that they be in behavior as becometh holiness, not false accusers, not given to much wine, teachers of good things; 4. That they may teach the young women to be sober, to love their husbands, to love their children, 5, to be discreet, chaste, keepers at home, good, obedient to their own husbands, that the word of God not be blasphemed.*"

With a focus on verses 3 through 5, the scripture is instructing more mature women to teach younger, inexperienced women how to conduct themselves not only in marriage but in life. This also emphasizes the importance of having mentors, both natural and spiritual. If you do not know what marriage looks like, seek out an aged (mature) married woman and spend time with her. Ask questions. If possible, observe her interactions with her husband – not in a creepy way, but pay attention. Then, the most important step, go to the Bible, because ultimately, this is where your instruction will be found. The Word of God provides wisdom, and observation helps with practical application.

Now, as I go into defining words and breaking down the scripture, anything in the New Testament is in Greek. Anything from the Old Testament is in Hebrew. Titus is in the New Testament, so all of the words I define will be from a Greek word. Verse one provides the purpose of what follows – to provide sound or uncorrupt instruction. Let's break down verses three through five. Verse three reads, "The aged women likewise, that they be in behavior as becometh holiness, not false accusers, not given to much wine, teachers of good things."

In verse 3, "aged women" is the word *presbutis*, which means aged woman or man, but it also comes from the Greek word *presbuteros,* or our English word, presbytery or elder, of age or rank. The word "behavior" is the Greek word *katastema*, which means a position or condition, that is, demeanor. It comes from a root word which means to place down, to designate, constitute, convoy: - appoint, be, conduct, make, ordain, set. "Becometh holiness" means just that – reverent or respectful. "False accuser" is the word *diabolos*, which means a traducer; specifically, Satan. In other words, making false accusations is satanic, which is one reason we should avoid it at all costs. "Not given to much wine" means what you may think it means – given means to enslave. In other words, do not be a slave to wine. I just want to free some people and say that it does not say you cannot have wine, it is saying do not overindulge.

"Teachers of good things" comes from two root words, *kalos* (of uncertain affinity or beautiful or morally good) and *didaskalos* (an instructor or to teach in a broad sense), which means literally instructor in that which is beautiful or morally good. Younger women can learn that from their more mature mentors.

Verse four means to teach young women to be sober, literally of sound mind, to discipline or correct. Younger women need older, godly women who can check and correct things in them at times, whether it be false doctrine or even if they see behavior that could be damaging to the young woman's marriage. I will talk about what some of those behaviors can include a bit later. This checking and correcting (whether direct or indirect) is necessary to teach younger women how to befriend their husbands and children. The word "love" in verse 4 is not the Greek word *agape,* which is indicative of the highest form of love, the love of God for man and man for God, nor *eros,* which is indicative of erotic or sensual love, but *philos,* which means friend, affectionate, or fond.

Let's dig into this *philos* relationship versus the other forms of love. **John 15:13** says, *"Greater love has no one than this, than to lay down one's life for his friends."* The word "love" is *agape*, but the word friend is *philos.* Therefore, God's love is exemplified in laying one's life[75] down for your friends or *philos.* The sacrifice involved in laying down soulish desires for your friend or love is linked to the love God has for us and vice versa. Jesus eventually called his disciples friends because he shared all he had with them. In marriage, you must be willing to share all that you are.

Even when things are challenging with my husband, and we are getting on each other's nerves, I remember, this is my friend.

---

[75] Life - the word life is the Greek word *psuche* which means breath or soul.

When we disagree, I remember, this is my friend. I would be remiss to make it seem as if I still don't say things that push his buttons or may hurt his feelings; sometimes I do. All of us have had situations where the words make their way out of our mouths before we can stop them. He knows me at my best, he knows me at my worst. He's been there when I was sick, in the hospital, and through childbirth. He has literally seen it all. And he has loved me through it all.

Verse 5 is a big one. Older women are to teach younger women to be discreet (sober-minded, temperate, not impulsive, to save, deliver, protect things of a sensitive nature); chaste (modest); keepers of the home (a good homemaker, from a root word which means to guard the home); good (in any sense, benefit); obedient to their own husband (submit self to) – and, this is important – that the word of God not be blasphemed (or defamed).

Everything in verses 3 through 5 is necessary to ensure the word of God is glorified. How, you may ask? A passage that comes to mind is **Ephesians 5:30-32**, in which Paul states: *"For we are members of his body, of his flesh, and of his bones. For this cause shall a man leave his father and mother and shall be joined unto his wife, and they two shall be one flesh. This is a great mystery: but I speak concerning Christ and the church."*

Just for background, in verses 22 to 32 of Ephesians 5, Paul details what the relationship between husbands and wives should be, and throughout, he relates it to the relationship Christ has with us, his church. If we doubted at all that this is where Paul was headed, he ties it up in verse 32. Our marriages are to follow the relationship between Christ and his church. In doing so, we glorify God in the earth and show His word to be true. Marriage is serious to God, and He likens the marriage of man and woman to the relationship Christ has with each of us individually and corporately as His body.

Building Your House

Proverbs 14:1 KJV:

1. Every wise woman buildeth her house: but the foolish plucketh it down with her hands.

Proverbs 14:1 MSG:

1. Lady Wisdom builds a lovely home; Sir Fool comes along and tears it down brick by brick.

As an undergraduate, one of my majors was Psychology. One of the models I studied was Tuckman's Stages of Group Development. They involve five stages – forming, storming, norming, performing, and adjourning (sometimes referred to as mourning). You're probably thinking, aren't we talking about marriage? Yes, we are.

When you first meet your mate, you are in the forming stage. This is the courtship phase and can leak into the beginning of the marriage. You're excited about the potential of the relationship and getting to know one another. You are on your best behavior, you are polite, pleasant – the best version of yourself. Your mate has just met your representative. You are Flo from Progressive. Everything is lovely, and you may not disagree much, or at all.

You may have seen a bit of the good, the bad, the ugly, and the indifferent. You feel in your heart, this is the one. You decide to get married. Then comes the storming stage. Some of the excitement has begun to wear off. You aren't Flo anymore, you are Florence Ann from Waxahachie, Texas. The weight of the commitment may set in. Dear One, you have realized this is forever, ever and your honey from State Farm who gave you flowers and "Good morning" texts, well, he farts in his sleep, and it stinks… a lot. He pronounces the "L" in salmon. This is still your beau, but now, your guards are down. The representatives have gone back to headquarters, and the real you has emerged.

You may think the storming stage is negative. As crazy as it sounds, it isn't at all. It can be a big positive. The storming stage and how you and your partner weather it can strengthen your relationship. As uncomfortable as it is, storming is healthy. Staying in the storming stage indefinitely is not healthy. This takes us back to our base scripture. Will you use the mud and straw and general mess that can seem to come from this storming stage to make bricks, or will you pull up the foundation which has already been laid?

I remember one of the first disagreements with my husband. I can't remember what the disagreement was about, but I remember how I felt. In our time, dating or courting, we never had an argument. I was in unfamiliar territory. I did not know how to properly deal with conflict, and I was so sad afterward.

I thought he was going to leave me. I was despondent because, in my mind, I had failed.

He asked me what was wrong, and I think I asked him if he wanted to leave me, or I told him I was afraid he would leave. He looked at me like I had two heads. Of course, he was not going anywhere, but I needed that reassurance. By sharing my fears and being vulnerable in those moments of storming, we were able to take the mess, make bricks, and build. Fears could be put to rest, and we could move on to the next stage – norming.

The norming stage is when a group begins to find its stride. Trust and confidence have been established, and the conflict has brought the parties closer. This can feel comfortable after the discomfort of the storming stage. And it appears that you could just stay in this stage forever and avoid the things that brought on the storming stage. And in theory, you can. However, in doing so, you risk sacrificing the goals God had in mind when He brought you together. The norming stage seems like a great place to stay, but be careful, inertia or lack of forward movement can occur.

Next is the performing stage. If you can push past the apparent peace and comfort of the norming stage, God can truly perform exploits with you and your spouse as a unit. This is where common goals such as a home, advancement in career or education, or expansion of your group, i.e., children, can begin to be accomplished. You are beginning to come into a deep understanding and knowledge of one another. Hopefully, you were great friends before you got married, but now you are best friends. You and your spouse are submitted to God and to one another. You allow the Holy Spirit to be an active participant in your marriage.

Adjourning means completing the tasks the group had at

hand. In the context of marriage, the hope is always that your team or group will not adjourn until one or both of you go to heaven. Until that point, your union may go through the stages of storming, norming, and performing many more times as new life circumstances present themselves.

Let's circle back to our scripture, **Proverbs 14:1**. We have a decision to make each day – will we be Lady Wisdom or Sir Fool? Wisdom is defined in the dictionary as the quality of having experience, knowledge, and good judgment; the quality of being wise. Looking at the definition backward, the quality of being wise involves having experience, knowledge, and good judgment. Wisdom is built through our own experiences or gleaning from the experience, knowledge, and good judgment of others. Wisdom in the context of **Proverbs 14:1** is the Hebrew word *chakam*, which means to be wise (in mind, word, or act).

The word "build" in Proverbs is the Hebrew word *banah*, which means to build (literally and figuratively), begin to build, obtain children, make, repair, set (up), or build surely. The word "house" is *bayith* in Hebrew, which means a house (in the greatest variation of applications, especially a family, etc.), court, daughter, door, inside. But it also comes from the Hebrew word banah, which means to build. Both words have direct applications to family. Build = House = Family, and conversely, Family = House = Build. Family is your house, and your house must be built. It is a constant process. You cannot have a family without work, and you must work (build) to have a house and to have a family. The word build is literally in the house. You build the house from within, the foundation supports the house, and the foundation, for Christians, is Jesus the Christ.

Proverbs 14:1 also provides an explanation for the opposite –

the foolish or silly person plucks his or her house down. This is the Hebrew word *haras*, which means to pull down or in pieces, break, or destroy. The phrase "with her hands" is the word *yad*, which means power, means, direction, or strength. How crazy is that? We have the power or means to build, produce, and if we are not careful, to destroy or overthrow our own efforts to build.

Proverbs 14:3 states, *"In the mouth of the foolish is a rod of pride: but the lips of the wise shall preserve them."* In marriage, I have found that there is no room for a "rod," defined as a twig, of pride or arrogance in Hebrew. A twig is a small piece of a branch. So, not even a little bit of pride or arrogance is warranted if you consider yourself wise. Twigs of pride or arrogance can undermine efforts to build your house. The lips of the wise preserve or hedge about, guard, and protect. The word "preserve" in **Proverbs 14:3** is the same Hebrew word used for "keep" in **Genesis 2:15**, *shamar*. Let's look at **Genesis 2:15**, which states, *"And the Lord God took the man [Adam] and put him into the garden of Eden to dress it and to keep it."*

Adam was charged with keeping the garden. The word "garden" comes from a Hebrew word, *gan*, which is defined as a garden, but also an enclosed garden (figuratively of a bride). The root means to defend, cover, surround, or protect. Your marriage should be like the enclosed garden of Eden. God has placed both you and your husband within that space to preserve, defend, and protect it. Your marriage is an inner sanctum in which only God, you, and your spouse have access to the roots. In keeping your marriage, be sure to allow God to do some pruning, so both you and your mate flourish.

The Practice of Discretion

Proverbs 11:22 KJV:

22. As a jewel of gold in a swine's snout, so is a fair woman which is without discretion.

Proverbs 11:22 MSG:

22. Like a gold ring in a pig's snout is a beautiful face on an empty head.

In an earlier chapter, I mentioned practices that could be harmful to marriage. Lack of discretion is one of those practices. Discretion is a noun, and the dictionary defines it as the quality of behaving or speaking in such a way as to avoid causing offense or revealing private information. For the purposes of this discussion, I want to focus on the latter part of the definition. There are some things that are private and should remain between you and your spouse. If you lack discretion, you may make others privy to matters or incidents within your relationship that may cause them to look at you or your spouse differently and/or make an incomplete or faulty judgment about you, your spouse, or the situation.

Not sure what I mean? I will provide an example: You and your husband are discussing expanding your family. You are ready to start trying to conceive. Your spouse points out that you are both juggling a lot and may not be juggling well. Your husband suggests that maybe the two of you should wait a bit longer and get your house in order before bringing a child into the situation. In your hurt, you call your girlfriend and you tell her your husband does not want to give you a baby, and he thinks you cannot handle motherhood. A civil discussion between you and your husband now has a third party. And this third party is not working with an accurate portrayal of the situation. In your hurt, you have shared how you processed what your husband said, not what he actually said or meant.

This lack of discretion (and one could argue, manipulation of the situation) could breed further discord in your marriage. Instead of sharing with your spouse how those words made you feel, you shared it with your girlfriend. Now your friend does not have a complete picture of what happened or even how to properly counsel you if that was your initial purpose in sharing the information.

Discretion is the Hebrew word *ta'am*, which the Strong's Concordance states comes from a root that means to taste; figuratively to perceive. It also means judgment, reason, and understanding. Lack of discretion can create a problem with perception, judgment, reasoning, or understanding. Going back to the base scripture, a fair or beautiful woman without discretion is compared to gold jewelry in a swine's snout. In the Bible, swine are considered unclean animals and are not well regarded.[76] Basically, adding outward value to something that lacks it intrinsically. The Message version is much more blunt – it states the woman is a beautiful face on an empty head. Yikes.

A word of balance here – if there is abuse happening, this should be shared. Otherwise, seek God in prayer. Look in His Word for answers. And if you need advice on how to handle situations within marriage, this is when you may want to reach out to an elder, Christian woman, or counselor whom you trust. There are some things you may not want even your good girlfriends to know, and that is okay. If you have a good relationship with your pastor's wife (if your pastor is male) or your pastor (if your pastor is a woman) or a female elder in the church, you may seek them out for godly advice. If there is a situation that seems you and your husband cannot resolve, or you feel you need some objectivity present, I recommend scheduling counseling with your pastors or a Christian counselor.

The practice of discretion can provide a hedge of protection for your marriage. Satan hates marriage. Protect it, protect yourself, protect your husband.

---

[76] see **Leviticus 11:7** and **Luke 8:26-33**

Adding Value

Song of Solomon 1:15 KJV:

15. Behold, thou art fair, my love; behold, thou art fair; thou hast dove's eyes.

Hebrews 13:4 KJV:

4. Marriage is honorable in all, and the bed undefiled: but whoremongers and adulterers God will judge.

All women have a story. Some developed early, and some developed late. Some of us felt like ugly ducklings, some of us were bullied, some of us were the bullies. Some us were popular, some of us felt like we never fit in. But very few of us can say that we never had insecurity about our bodies and how men see us.

In working on this book, I thought of my husband and something he said that helped change my understanding of how he sees me, and it also healed something in me.

For me, I was always known for my backside or booty, to use a colloquial term. It always got attention. I spent years as a young girl, then a preteen, trying to hide it, make it less noticeable. As a teenager, I was not busty at all, but I had hips and a backside, and as a girl who suffered from a low opinion of my looks, I thought, well, at least I have that to attract men. Otherwise, I was stuck with my intellect, and I will be honest, people see you before they hear you.

I did not really start to see myself as beautiful until I got saved. What I did not realize was that I thought my backside was the main asset my husband was attracted to when we were intimate. One day, when I was playing around and turning my back to him, he said, "Baby, turn around, I think ALL of you is beautiful. I love ALL of you."

Even though I know God made me in His image, and I am beautiful, part of me still has that old mindset from girlhood up to adulthood. So, what I want to say is that ALL of you are beautiful. You are more than breasts, hips, lips, booty, and thighs. You are worthy of being loved as a whole. You are more than the sum of your parts.

In sharing that personal story, I want to go back to the scriptures. In Song of Solomon, seeing your spouse through a dove's eyes points to being intoxicated with them if you look at the Hebrew, the root for dove comes from a word that means wine. But it also points to seeing your love through the blood of Jesus. Wine is often equated with the blood of Jesus according to **1 Corinthians 11:23-25,** and the dove with the Holy Spirit according to **Matthew 3:16**.

Marriage also adds value to each party, the Bible says so in **Hebrews 13:4**. The word honorable comes from a Greek word that means valuable, costly, or honored. The root word means a value, that is, money paid. Many of us were still healing from our pasts, insecurities, or past abuses and violations when we entered marriage. The beautiful thing about it is that if we view one another through the eyes of the Holy Spirit, and we show one another grace, great healing can also come through the union. What I have learned is that marriage does not solve the problems or bring closure to the issues that were already there – in fact, it holds them up to a magnifying glass.

Marriage puts you in a position where you must face it, or it could harm the marriage. What I have also learned is that if you and your mate love Jesus, you will find it in yourselves to give one another the grace needed to mature and to heal. God will provide opportunities for you to see one another as He sees you. And here is the other piece I want to point out: he married you because you were already valuable. Your partner married you because he saw something in you that he wanted, and it was not just your body. **Proverbs 18:22** states, *"Whoso findeth a wife findeth a good thing, and obtaineth favor of the Lord."* When your husband married you, it literally pleased the Lord. The word favor comes from a root that means to be pleased with, specifically to satisfy a debt. God loves marriage; it delights Him.

Within the verse from Hebrews, it also speaks to sexuality in marriage. It is undefiled. Sex is clean within marriage. It should not make you feel dirty, nor deform you spiritually or physically. If you have issues surrounding sex, whether it be past abuses or violations that make you feel dirty, have an open and honest conversation with your spouse before you engage in sex again. It may be a situation in which your partner can reassure you, or it may be something you need to work through with a counselor, solo or together. Sex is a healthy part of marriage. It should be enjoyed by both of you. Seek the Lord, but also seek wise counsel if needed to make sure this part of marriage, which should be fun, does not become a chore or a "cross to bear."

The Proverbs 31 Woman in the 21st Century

~~~
&#8226;
~~~

Proverbs 31:10-31 Revised KJV:

10. Who can find a virtuous woman? for her price is far above rubies. **11.** The heart of her husband does safely trust in her, so that he will have no need of spoil. **12.** She will do him good and not evil all the days of her life. **13.** She seeks wool, and flax, and works willingly with her hands. **14.** She is like the merchants' ships; she brings her food from afar. **15.** She rises also while it is yet night, and gives meat to her household, and a portion to her maidens. **16.** She considers a field, and buys it: with the fruit of her hands she plants a vineyard. **17.** She girds her loins with strength, and strengthens her arms. **18.** She perceives that her merchandise is good: her candle goes not out by night. **19.** She lays her hands to the spindle, and her hands hold the distaff. **20.** She stretches out her hand to the poor; yea, she reaches forth her hands to the needy. **21.** She is not afraid of the snow for her household: for all her household are clothed with scarlet. **22.** She makes herself coverings of tapestry; her clothing is silk and purple. **23.** Her husband is known in the gates, when he sits among the elders of the land. **24.** She makes fine linen, and sells it; and delivers girdles unto the merchants. **25.** Strength and honor are her clothing; and she will rejoice in time to come. **26.** She opens her mouth with wisdom; and in her tongue is the law of kindness. **27.** She looks well to the ways of her household, and eats not the bread of idleness. **28.** Her children arise up, and call her blessed; her husband also, and he praises her. **29.** Many daughters have done virtuously, but you excel them all. **30.** Favor is deceitful, and beauty is vain: but a woman that fears the LORD, she will be praised. **31.** Give her of the fruit of her hands; and let her own works praise her in the gates.

I think often, the idea of an independent, strong woman, in the time we are in, is not synonymous with being a married woman. Think about popular songs and movies – how many of those strong, independent women are married? I'll wait. In a high-level overview of the **Proverbs 31** woman, we learn a few things: a virtuous woman is extremely valuable for a man to have. She is someone her husband trusts with his heart, his inner thoughts, he does not need a woman on the side.

She does good for him all the days of her life. She seeks out means of helping to provide for her family, clothing, and food. She gets up early to make sure she has a meal prepared for her whole household. She has her own money to buy a field she wants to plant a vineyard[77]. She practices restraint. She knows

---

[77] lit. another stream of income

that what she has is good. She is constantly looking for ways to produce, even making clothes on the spindle. She is altruistic, she helps the poor and those with less.

She is not afraid when hard times come because her family is clothed in scarlet [the blood of Jesus]. She is royalty [clothing is silk and purple]. Her husband is well-regarded amongst the elders. She is strong and beautiful and full of wisdom. But not only that, she is also very kind. She is always looking after her household, she is not idle. Her children and her husband praise her and call her blessed. She fears the Lord, and because of that, she is praised, or she shines.

I've paraphrased, but let's look at the scripture. The word virtuous means strength, might, efficiency, wealth, army, and force. So literally, the Hebrew asks, *"Who can find a strong woman? For her price* [value] *is far above rubies* [a precious stone]?" The Bible does not set women up as weak; no, it is good to be strong, in fact, this is what makes a woman valuable! Her strength is found in the verses which follow. Her husband can trust her with the deep parts of himself, which he may only share with her and God. She deals well with him, she is not unpleasant, and does not do anything to hurt him. She is a woman of discretion! She is a woman who takes care of her household, but is also a go-getter! She has multiple streams of income. She is not afraid to help others, but notice, her first ministry is to her husband and her home.

In our society, it is not uncommon for a woman to make more money than her husband or be an entrepreneur. The woman in **Proverbs 31** had her own money! She used her own money to plant a vineyard from which her family would reap the increase. Listen, I really need you to get this! We do not know if she made more money than her husband, but it does not matter because how she carried herself was a credit to him. He was well-respected among the elders. She is out here buying vineyards, making clothes, and selling merchandise.

So even if you are an entrepreneur or you make more money than your husband, your submission is required. He is still your covering, and Jesus is still his covering. That order does not get usurped based on what you bring into the home financially. Just as Sarah called Abraham, *"Lord, Lord,"* we are to respect our husbands in the same manner. I could dive deeper, but my point in referencing this is to show this extraordinary woman is not unlike you and I. We may not be just like her, but she is a standard that we can strive toward. She is a woman of discretion who is loved and respected by her husband, children, and others she encounters. She contributes to her household. We should aim to do the same.

About the Author

Dameon Gibbs holds an BA in Anthropology and World History and an MA in Classical Studies. For the past five years he has worked with inner-city youth in Baltimore, Maryland. He has been an avid writer since his days in high school during the late 1990's. He enjoys the creative process of all writing genres, whether it be religious, poetic, science fiction, historical, biographies or action adventure.

Dameon is married to fellow author Tiffany Michele.

Tiffany Gibbs, who also writes under the name Tiffany Michele, is an author who crosses genres. Whether it be nonfiction, science fiction, or poetry, Tiffany enjoys it all. She enjoys writing books for children, as well as for young adults, and adult readers. Her love of reading started early and grew as she began to craft her own stories from an early age. She aims to encourage, inspire, and educate in her stories.

Based out of Baltimore, Tiffany is originally from Virginia Beach, VA.

You can connect with me on:

🌐 https://gibbspublishingconglomerate.com
🅕 https://www.facebook.com/GibbsPublishing
🔗 https://www.instagram.com/gibbspubs/#

Also by Dameon Gibbs

He has been an avid writer since his days in high school during the late 1990s. He enjoys the creative process of all writing genres, whether it be religious, poetic, science fiction, historical, biographies, or action-adventure.

Children of the Kingdom: Walking In Your Royal Lineage
Jesus the Christ made it very clear in Matthew 18:3, stating we must become as little children to enter the kingdom of heaven. In this book, we will examine characteristics of children, using them as a lens through which we must look to truly understand our Heavenly Father. With a child's mind, we get to grow into our own, take our position as heirs, rule with authority, and trust in God's ability to father us.

Unrelenting: Becoming a Warrior

Over the days, months, years, and centuries, the enemies of God have been spoiling the church. They have taken health, happiness, wealth, children, marriages, lives, peace, and faith. But now the stronger than he has come, and He (Christ) has given His people the means to retrieve their spoils. No more does the church have to take the beating it had been receiving. The Church is called to a higher purpose of power and dominion, a power that gives dominion over all that can be thrown at it. This book will discuss how the church must expect to be victorious in all things. By the spirit of God, we must change our minds from being a victim to that of an unrelenting and honorable warrior.

Jesus You Are...

The Bible says that everything that believers do should speak of Jesus. With that, I believe that everything that we learn should give honor to our Lord, including our language. This book was written to help children learn about our Messiah through the use of the alphabet.

Seven Biblical Principles of Success

God wants all His people to be successful spiritually and naturally. He has given us a written guideline and format to help bring about that success. The purpose of this book is to focus on how we can be successful as a whole, successful in our minds, our spirituality, our bodies, and within our families. Using the Book of Genesis, this book discusses seven biblical principles that, if applied, will help bring about the success God desires us all to attain.

Words To My God

God takes the broken pieces of this vessel and makes me whole day by day. This is the expression of my brokenness, my reconstruction, and the process. Every walk is different, but I hope you find encouragement in my journey.

"In the day of thy power, and the beauties of holiness from the womb of the morning: thou hast the dew of thy youth," Psalms 110:3

Found In The Storm

Found in the Storm by Tiffany and Dameon Gibbs is a gripping fictional narrative that seamlessly weaves together themes of betrayal, forgiveness, redemption, survival, and the testing of one's faith.

The protagonist, Antonio, is a character whose perilous journey forms the backbone of the story. He is a very complex individual with strengths and flaws. His decision to join the Army with the hope of improving his life, only to face a dishonorable discharge, sets the stage for a series of challenges that test his resilience and determination. The story cleverly explores the complexities of Antonio's life as he navigates the aftermath of his choices.

The plot takes a turn when Antonio accepts an under-the-table job flying a helicopter, reminiscent of his military days. The seemingly straightforward task of transporting a package from point A to point B in rural Minnesota becomes a high-stakes adventure, especially when a deadly winter storm sweeps in. The authors create a palpable sense of tension and suspense as Antonio grapples with the decision to risk his life for what initially appeared to be easy money. Will he be able to successfully navigate the helicopter through the blinding, severe snowstorm? How will he survive being on the brink of death?

Found in the Storm is a must-read for those who enjoy traversing the twists and turns of a story with a compelling blend of adventure and suspense. This novel will leave a lasting impact, inviting readers to reflect on the intricate tapestry of life and the choices that shape our destinies.